THE OFFICIAL LEGO® NINJAGO™ ANNUAL 2017

CONTENTS

MATCHING MACHINE

How well do you know the Masters of Spinjitzu? Probably better than this machine does! It was supposed to match the pictures of the ninja with their descriptions, but it got mixed up. Fix the machine's mistakes and write the correct number and letter below each ninja's name opposite.

1

2

3

A

B

C

LLOYD
He's the Gold Ninja but still wears green.

KAI
His costume is the colour of fire.

JAY
His favourite colour is blue.

LLOYD

KAI

JAY

NYA

COLE

ZANE

4

5

6

D

E

F

NYA
The only girl in the ninja team.

COLE
The only ninja with a green face.

ZANE
He looks at you with a robotic eye.

WEAPON WATCH!

Master Wu wants you to keep an eye on the ninja weapons. Look carefully at the first column on the left, then mark the new weapons that have appeared in the second and third columns.

1

2

3

PIRATE CREW

The evil, wish-granting djinn Nadakhan has brought his pirate crew to Ninjago world. Can you find their names in the grid? Watch out – one of them is missing! Mark the missing pirate's picture.

CLANCEE

DOUBLOON

DOGSHANK

FLINTLOCKE

SQIFFY

CYREN

BUCKO

MONKEY WRETCH

F	L	I	B	U	C	K	O	C	K
A	A	Z	A	S	C	L	A	L	N
D	O	U	B	L	O	O	N	A	W
S	U	D	O	G	S	H	A	N	K
Q	S	A	C	Y	D	R	G	C	Y
I	A	T	S	A	C	Y	R	R	N
F	O	D	P	U	C	P	O	E	R
F	L	I	N	T	L	O	C	K	E
Y	A	H	J	T	B	P	A	C	I

CELEBRITY FEAST

FIRE!

Cyren is testing how powerful the pirate catapult is. Count up how many of each different brick she has fired and write the total numbers in the boxes below.

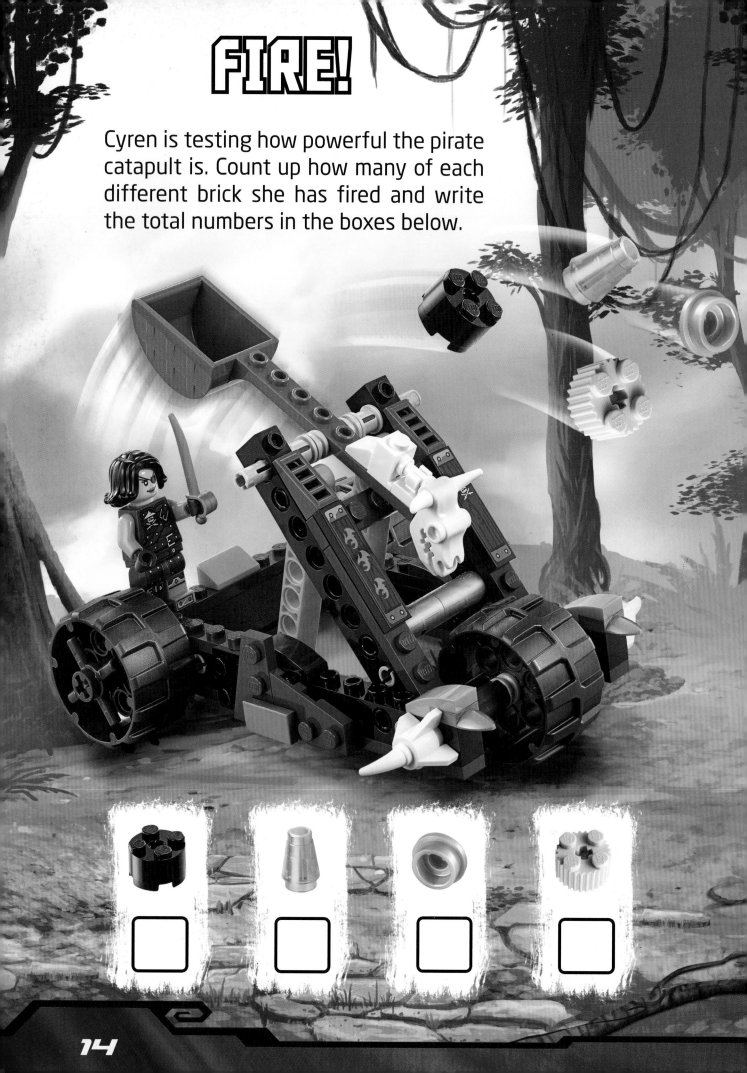

BATTLE MACHINE

Doubloon's Raid Zeppelin is perfectly designed for air strikes. Look at the Sky Pirate's flying machine and match the names to the parts.

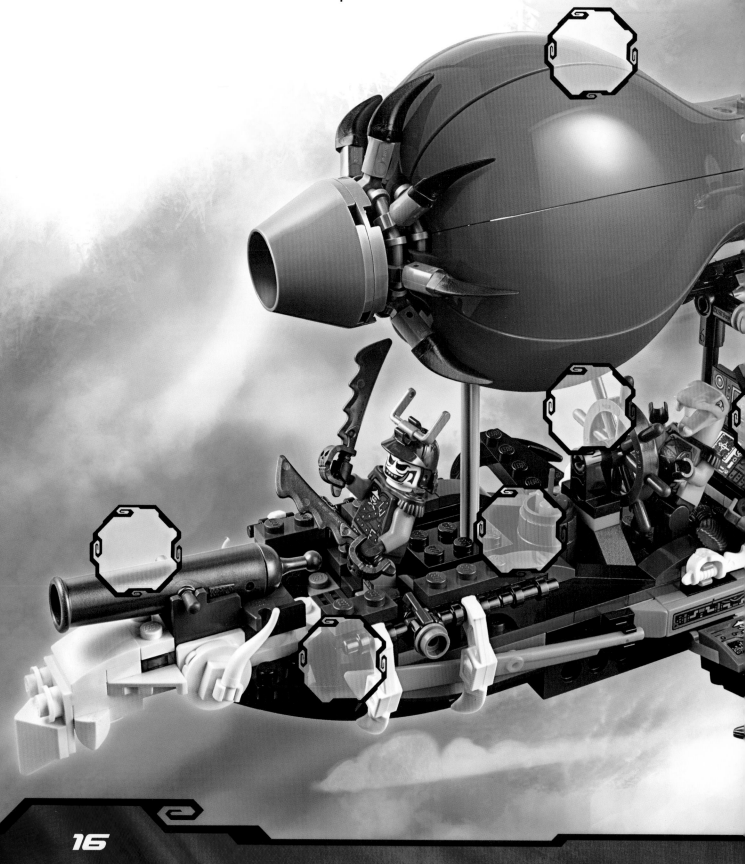

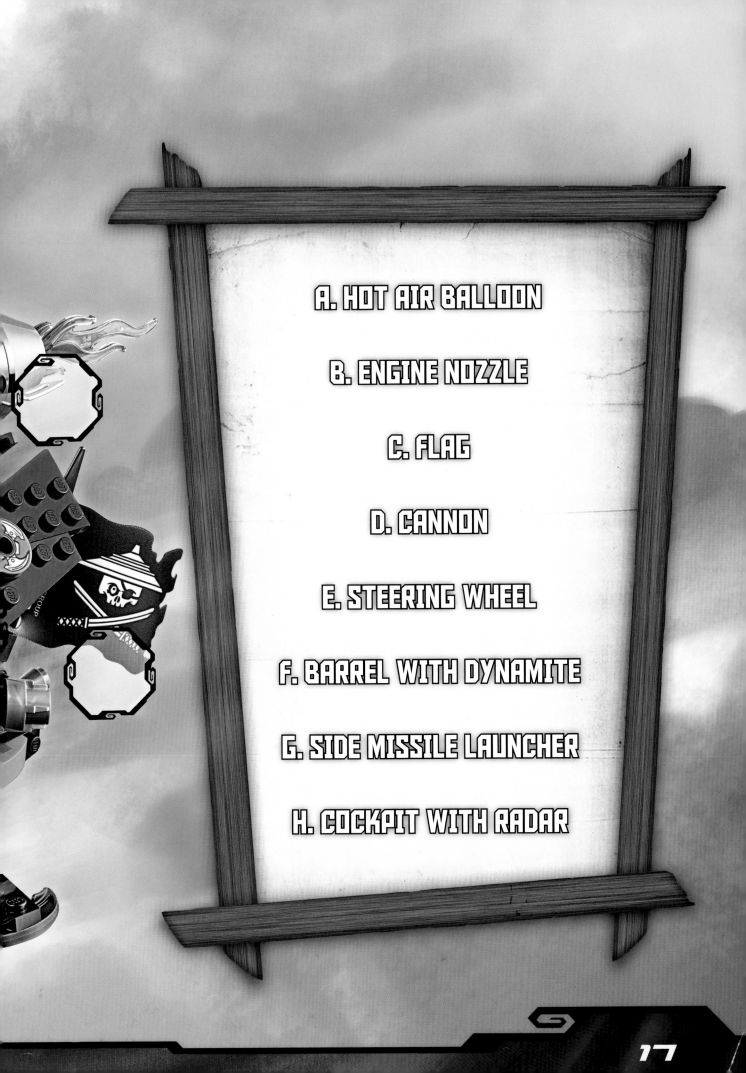

A. HOT AIR BALLOON

B. ENGINE NOZZLE

C. FLAG

D. CANNON

E. STEERING WHEEL

F. BARREL WITH DYNAMITE

G. SIDE MISSILE LAUNCHER

H. COCKPIT WITH RADAR

WANNABE FUGITIVE

Kryptarium prison is no place for the ninja. The heroes are planning to break free. Find out who wants to escape from the prison with them. Count the symbols around the characters. The one with the largest amount is the wannabe fugitive.

PRISON ESCAPE

Help Zane, Captain Soto and their fellow fugitive escape from Kryptarium prison! Guide them through the prison yard to Kai, but stay out of sight of the cameras. If they travel within the camera range, the alarm will be triggered!

START

FINISH

CAMERA RANGE:

FENCING LESSON

During an intensive sword fighting lesson, the ninja destroyed this poster of the Sky Pirate ship. Can you put it back together ready for another training session? Write the numbers of the pieces in the right places.

PIRATE CHALLENGE

Nadakhan has sent Sqiffy on a spying mission to Ninjago City. Which of the pictures on the opposite page is the mirror reflection of Sqiffy flying his winged vehicle?

1

2

3

4

WHO'S MISSING?

These dice have pictures of the Sky Pirates on them. They should all be the same, but some of the pictures are missing. Finish the dice by writing the correct numbers on the empty sides.

1

2

3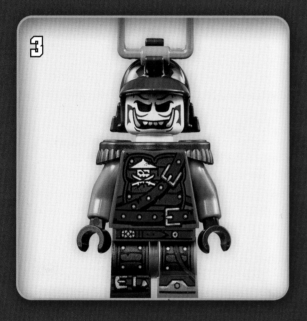

4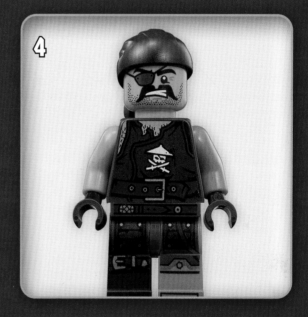

5

6

GENERAL OVERHAUL

Monkey Wretch is the fastest mechanic in Nadakhan's crew ... and the only mechanic! How fast can you do a general overhaul of *Misfortune's Keep*? Write the correct numbers in the spaces below to replace the ship's old parts with the new ones shown opposite.

MYSTERY LAIR

Cole is flying to Tiger Widow Island to find a giant spider's lair, but he's lost his way in the clouds. Help him complete his mission by discovering where he is.

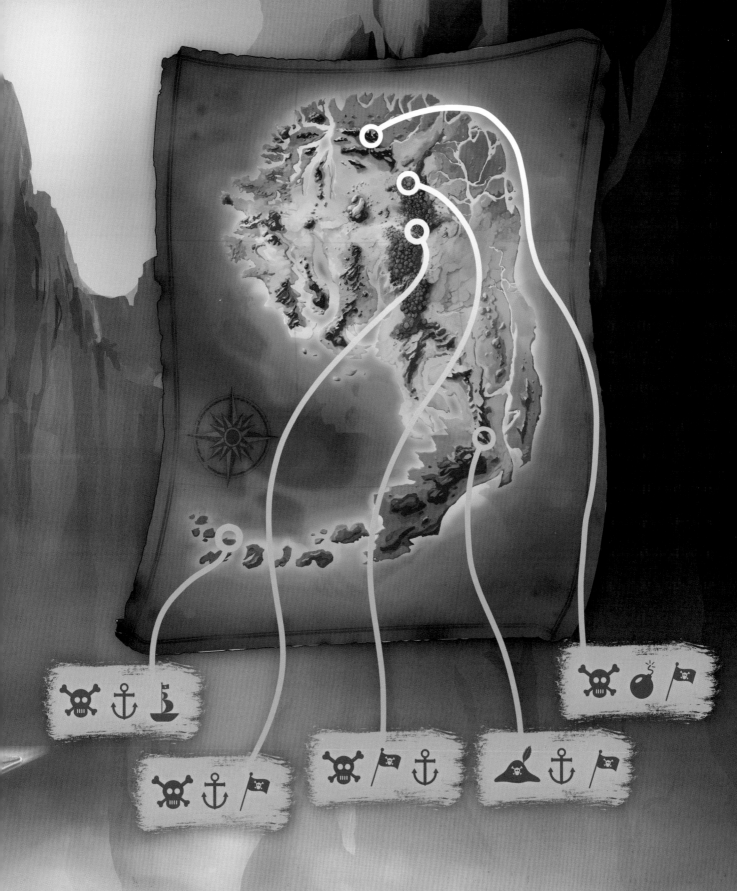

CLUE: Three symbols that look exactly like the ones on the opposite page mark Cole's position above Ninjago Island.

SCARY BEAST

The only thing that can help defeat the evil djinn is venom from a giant spider called Tiger Widow. But the beast won't give away its venom without a fight! Help Jay complete his mission by choosing the line that will lead him to the giant spider.

A   B   C

FOOLPROOF TRAP

AIR SUPPORT

The Sky Pirates are trying to stop the ninja from getting the venom. Guide Master Wu through the maze, so that he can get to Tiger Widow Island and help the ninja fight their opponents.

START

FINISH

THE DRAGONS' WARM-UP

The ninja are preparing for their next battle with the Sky Pirates – the mighty dragons are soaring through the air! Look carefully at the scene and mark two of the smaller pictures that do not belong to it.

DOMINO MASTERS

The Masters of Spinjitzu love playing dominoes! Use the tiles at the bottom of the page to complete the missing sections of the domino chain. Remember, the characters on the new tiles need to match the characters that come before and after on the existing tiles.

40

QUICK FIX

Nya and Jay have found a prototype of Zane in an old lighthouse. The old nindroid could help them fight the Sky Pirates, but they need to activate it first! Fix the torn wires by connecting the ends on the left to those on the right, so that each one adds up to ten.

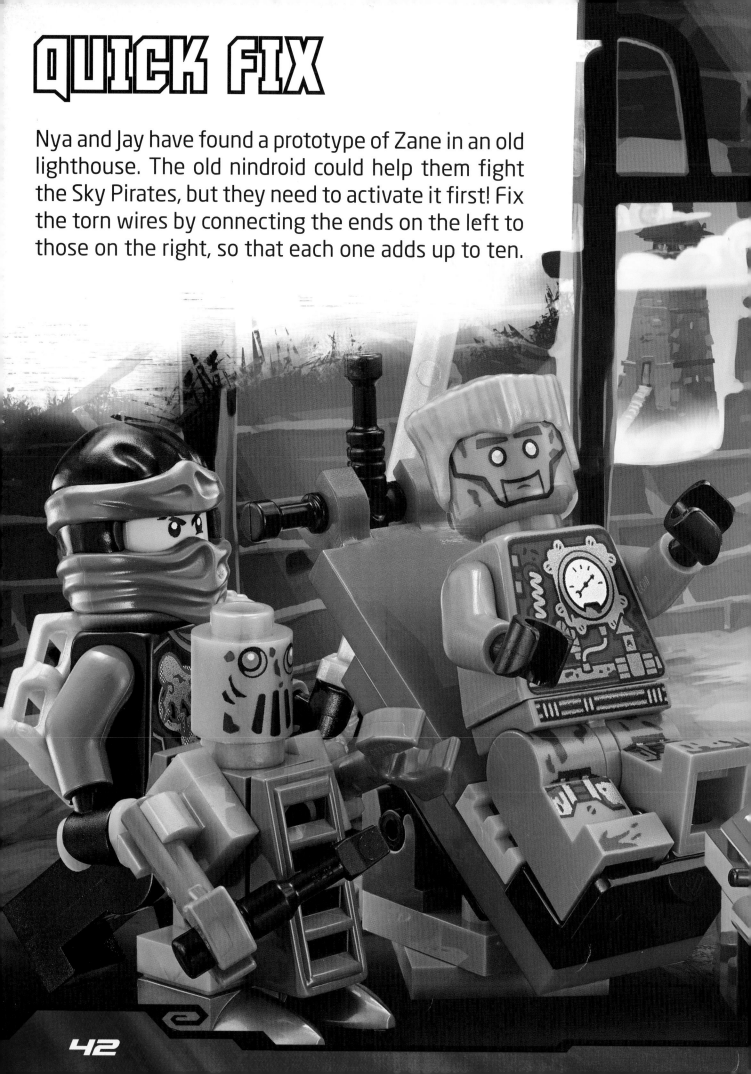

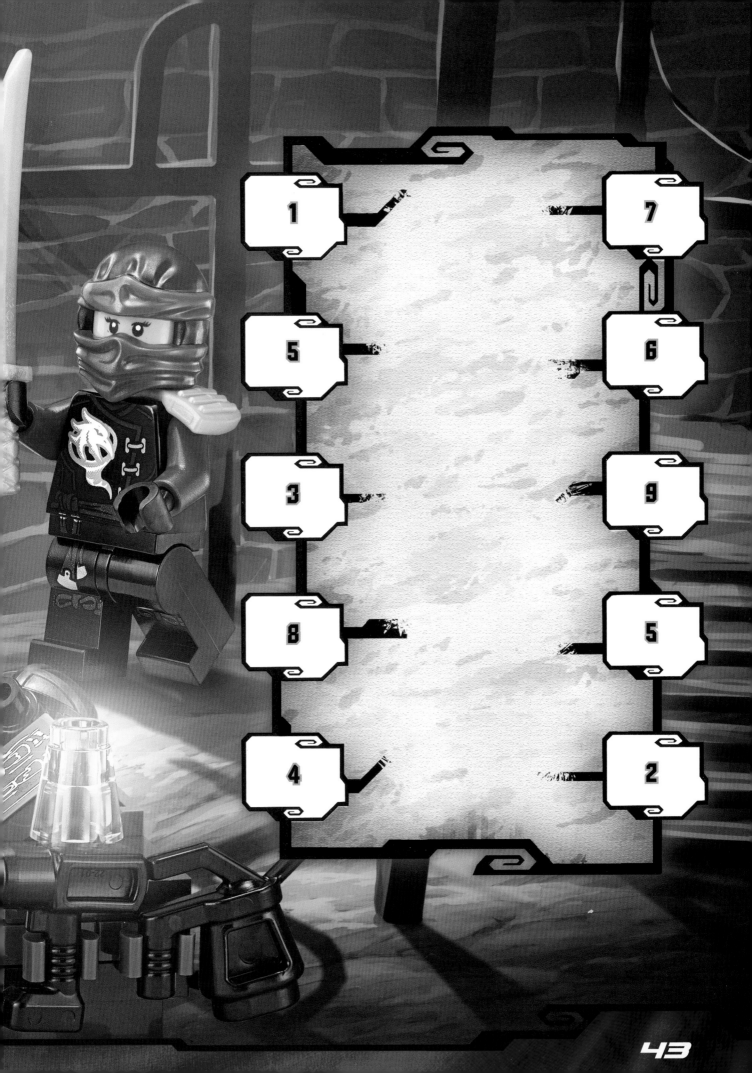

1

7

5

6

3

9

8

5

4

2

PIRATE ATTACK!

The Sky Pirates have laid siege to the lighthouse! The ninja are fighting hard, but Nadakhan's evil crew won't let go until they're defeated.

It seems that good fortune has smiled on the ninja! Look at these two pictures and spot eleven differences between them.

SKY PIRATE CLASH

Misfortune's Keep is the Sky Pirates' biggest and most powerful airship. Look at the battle the ninja are fighting on board the ship and mark which sentences are true and which are false.

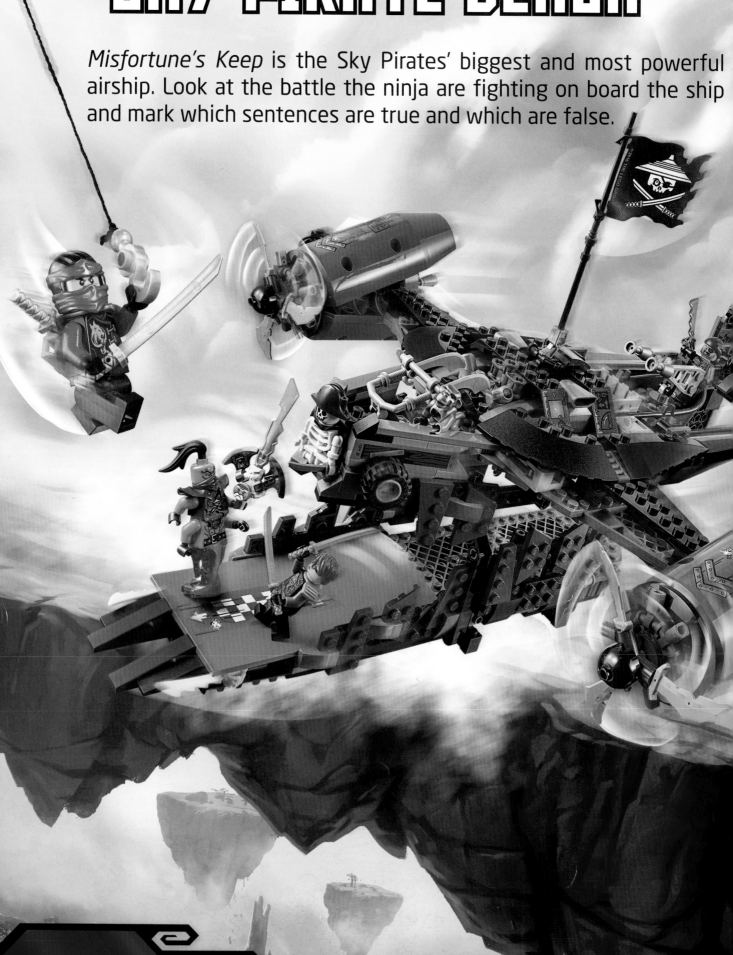

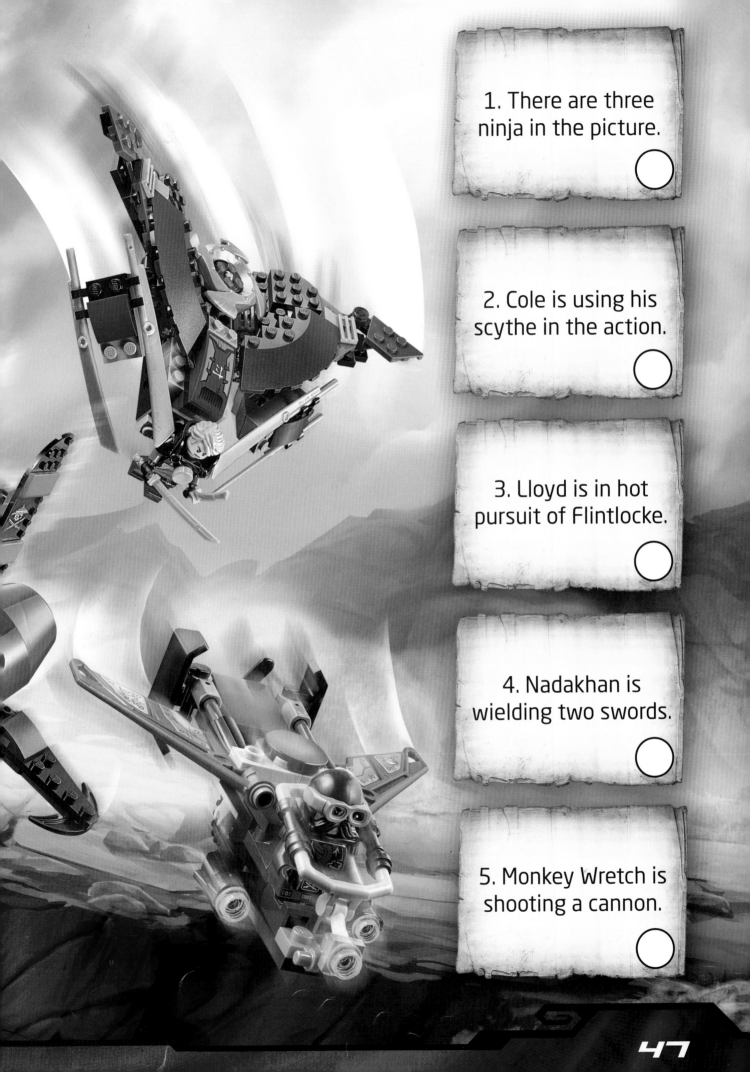

1. There are three ninja in the picture. ◯

2. Cole is using his scythe in the action. ◯

3. Lloyd is in hot pursuit of Flintlocke. ◯

4. Nadakhan is wielding two swords. ◯

5. Monkey Wretch is shooting a cannon. ◯

HIDDEN MACHINE

Lloyd can't tell which flying machine is his in the darkness. Look at the ships and help the ninja find the one that looks the same as the machine he is thinking about.

THE MISSING DETAIL

Look carefully at the picture of the ninja on their bikes. The four pictures on the opposite page are almost identical. Can you circle the space where one thing is missing from each one?

These bikes can't fly! How are we supposed to fight the Sky Pirates?

A

B

C

D

COIN COUNT

Is Ronin coming to help the ninja fight the Sky Pirates? No, he's too busy counting his money! Help him get his coins in order by writing their numbers in the correct places. If you're fast enough, Ronin might still find time to help his friends. Remember, each coin must only appear once in any row or column.

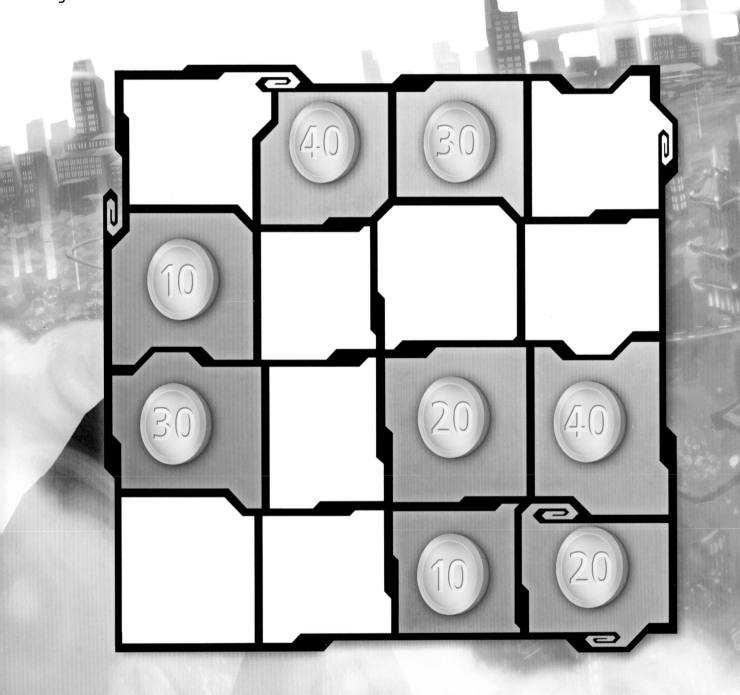

10 20 30 40

RACE TO SKY SHARK

Nothing beats an opportunity to sit behind *Sky Shark's* steering wheel! Who will be the lucky one today? Add the numbers along the lines leading from each pirate to the air ship. The smallest total will reveal who will pilot the vessel.

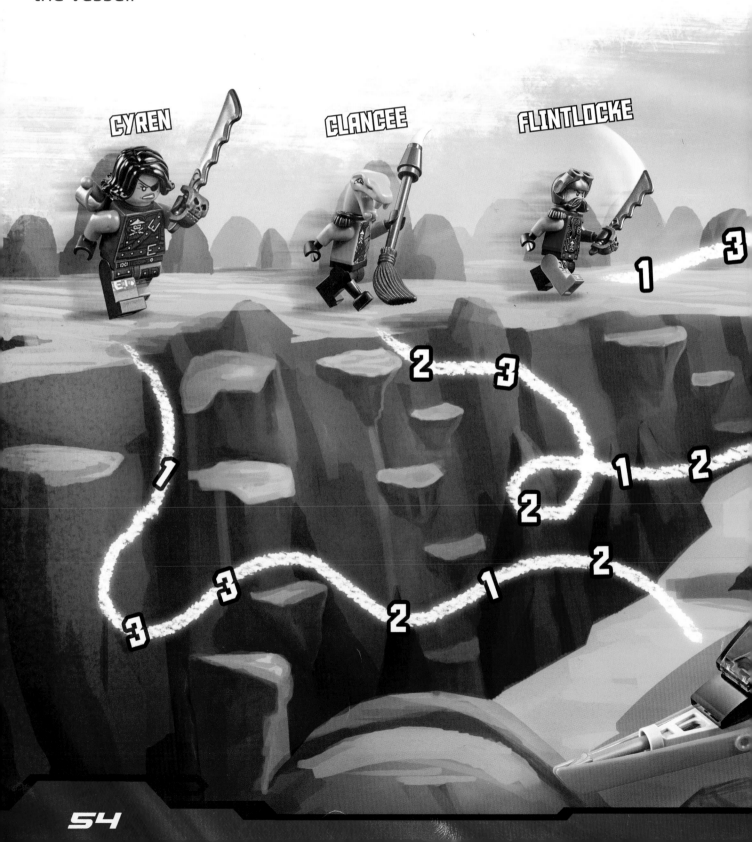

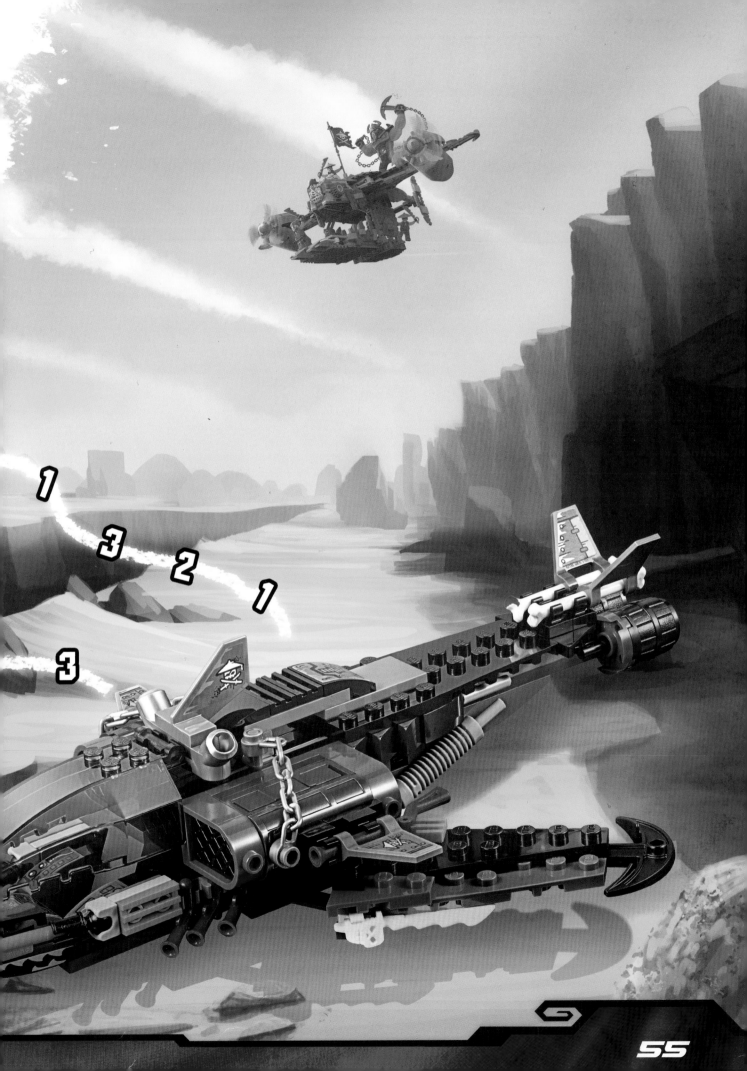

1

3

2

1

3

DJINN ARMY

Nadakhan conjured up lots of images of himself, but not all of them are perfect. Look closely at the djinn army and spot three that are different from the others.

ANSWERS

PAGES 6-7
MATCHING MACHINE

LLOYD – 5 AND C

KAI – 6 AND B

JAY – 4 AND E

NYA – 3 AND A

COLE – 1 AND D

ZANE – 2 AND F

PAGES 8-9
WEAPON WATCH!

 2

 3

PAGES 14-15
FIRE!

| 8 | 9 | 9 | 8 |

PAGES 10-11
PIRATE CREW
MONKEY WRETCH IS MISSING

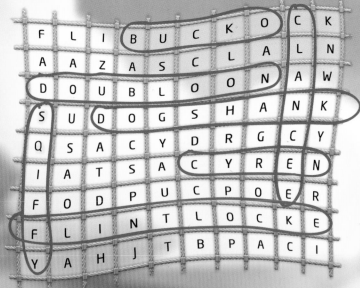

F	L	I	B	U	C	K	O	C	K
A	A	Z	A	S	C	L	A	L	N
D	O	U	B	L	O	O	N	A	W
S	U	D	O	G	S	H	A	N	K
Q	S	A	C	Y	D	R	G	C	Y
I	A	T	S	A	C	Y	R	E	N
F	O	D	P	U	C	P	O	E	R
F	L	I	N	T	L	O	C	K	E
Y	A	H	J	T	B	P	A	C	I

PAGES 16-17
BATTLE MACHINE

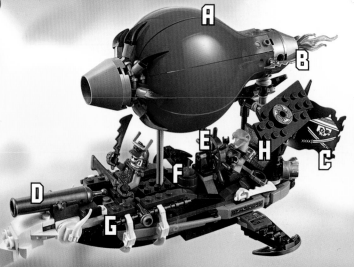

PAGES 18-19
WANNABE FUGITIVE

CAPTAIN SOTO   4

PAGES 20-21
PRISON ESCAPE

START

FINISH

PAGES 22-23
FENCING LESSON

7   9

1

5   6

8

2

4

3   10

PAGES 24-25
PIRATE CHALLENGE

4

PAGES 26-27
WHO'S MISSING?

A - 3   B - 6   C - 1

PAGES 28-29
GENERAL OVERHAUL

1

3

4

6

5

2

PAGES 30-31
MYSTERY LAIR

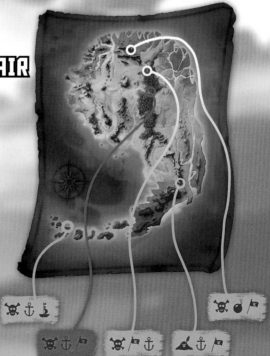

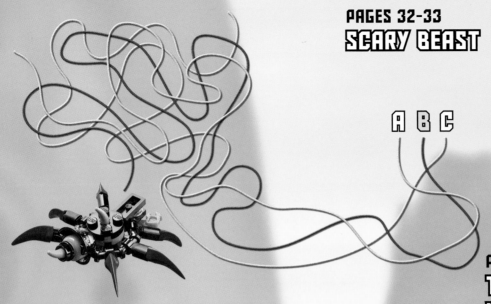

PAGES 32-33
SCARY BEAST

A B C

PAGES 38-39
THE DRAGONS' WARM-UP

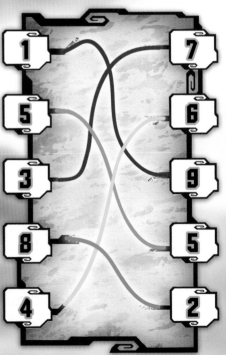

1   6

PAGES 36-37
AIR SUPPORT

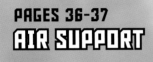

START

FINISH

PAGES 42-43
QUICK FIX

1   7

5   6

3   9

8   5

4   2

PAGES 40-41
DOMINO MASTERS

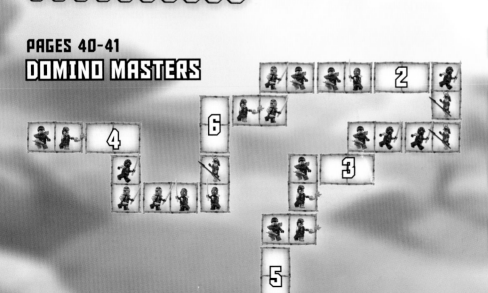

4   6   2

3

5

PAGES 44-45
PIRATE ATTACK!

PAGES 46-47
SKY PIRATE CLASH

1 - TRUE, 2 - FALSE, 3 - TRUE,

4 - FALSE, 5 - FALSE.

PAGES 50-51
THE MISSING DETAIL

PAGES 48-49
HIDDEN MACHINE

3

PAGES 52-53
COIN COUNT

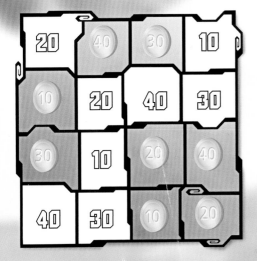

PAGES 56-57
DJINN ARMY

PAGES 54-55
RACE TO *SKY SHARK*
FLINTLOCKE

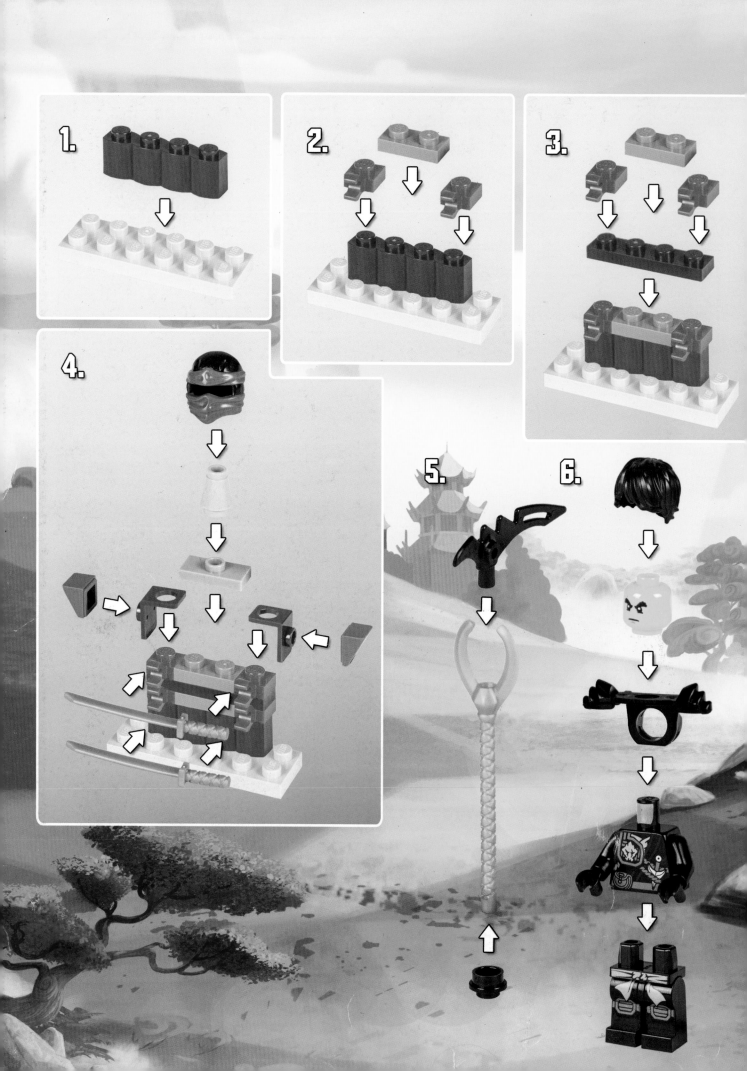